D1255183

HOW I
CHANGED MY
THINKING ABOUT
THE CHURCH

OTHER BOOKS

HOW I CHANGED MY THINKING ABOUT THE CHURCH

RICHARD C. HALVERSON

ZONDERVAN PUBLISHING HOUSE
A DIVISION OF THE ZONDERVAN CORPORATION
GRAND RAPIDS, MICHIGAN

Printed in the United States of America

Dedication

To the members, officers and associates of
Fourth Presbyterian Church in Bethesda,
Maryland, brothers and sisters in Christ, who
for the past 13 years have ministered to me
personally and through whom God has led me in
my way of thinking about the church.

Contents

Foreword

These are days of revolution. Seemingly there are just two classes of people—the oppressors and the oppressed. These are days of racism. No one with a mind and heart sensitive to the day in which we live can deny this. These are corrupt days— violent, secular, materialistic; and in our time we are seeing the bankruptcy of the best that men have tried to do to solve these problems: the failure of legislation—important as it is; the failure of education—important as it is; and even the failure of the church.

With the failure of the church has come the decision on the part of many that if any of these problems are to be resolved, they have to be resolved by organizations and institutions outside the church. As a result, in the last ten years we have seen developed many extra-church and extra-

9

religious organizations designed to attack racism, to stand with the oppressed against the oppressor and even in some cases if necessary, to wage violent revolution. Some of these organizations have even pledged to destroy the institutions and the systems that have supported the oppressor against the oppressed, that have supported, or at least have not resisted, racism.

From the outside these extra-church organizations have continually appealed to and expected from the Christian community the finances to subsidize their programs which have been run without responsibility to the Christian community, and when the support is not forthcoming, they have been exceedingly critical of the Christian community.

It is my thesis that the Christian community represents the chief resource for all the efforts to oppose oppression and racism. The Christian community represents an incalculable reservoir of human as well as financial resource to meet the needs in the inner city, to oppose the forces which oppress and demean and dehumanize. If the church has failed tragically, however, the answer is not to abandon her. Certainly these Christian communities are not going to respond to the incredible opportunity and accept their Christian responsibility if they are rejected by leadership instead of helped to see this responsibility and motivated to respond.

The writer of this book sees in the local Christian community, a most exciting opportunity to meet the challenge of our day. He sees the pastor of the local church as standing in a most strategic position to supply the resources and to supply even those organizations and movements which are attempting to solve social problems outside the Christian community. He believes there is a way to work within a local congregation so that congregation will comprehend its Christian duty to the world of need beyond and to respond to that Christian duty in ways that are relevant, significant and strategic.

This book is written in the light of human and social need today and in the immeasurable potential of the local Christian community as an incalculable resource to meet that need.

There is no greater challenge today to a servant of Christ than to pastor a local congregation, make it aware of its accountability to Jesus Christ, and motivate the members of that congregation as servants of God and man to address themselves to the massive needs everywhere.

Acknowledgment

I want to express appreciation to my secretary, Mrs. Winnie Mitchell, who has typed the manuscript and has been kind enough to do some editing in the process.

THINKING ABOUT THE CHURCH

Chapter 1

Thinking About the Church

The way a pastor thinks about the church which he serves determines what that church is to become. This has been a growing and deepening conviction in my experience as a pastor over the past ten years. I am not talking about his theology of the church but of the practical way he thinks about the church in the day-to-day affairs—in his prayers, in his relationships with his associates if he has any, with the officers of the church and with the people of the church. What he thinks about the church in this day-to-day, hour-by-hour practical way determines what the church will become.

I have seen this happen since coming to Fourth Presbyterian Church in Bethesda, Maryland in 1958. Having been out of the conventional pastorate for many years, I did not begin in Fourth

15

Church with a program which I could hardly wait to institute; I did not come with innovations or with a head full of plans to impose on the congregation as soon as possible. I simply came to pastor the church, believing it was God's will, and the only conviction I held was that perhaps, inasmuch as I had been involved in small group work, my ministry would express itself in this way.

However, this did not happen in the early years and though I tried every way I knew to start small groups, they did not seem to develop. In a mild frustration, as I prayed about this, it seemed that God gave me a vision of a congregation that in itself would have all the elements of the small group—a congregation where the people would really love one another, where they would be conscious of their accountability to each other in the Lord, their priestly responsibilities, their responsibility to minister to one another as well as to the world outside. It would be a caring congregation, a loving congregation, a congregation that would literally demonstrate the reconciliation which it professed.

This vision gripped me early in my ministry and I began to talk and to preach about it. As associates were added, they were encouraged to think this way about the church, to be people-centered rather than program-centered in their approach, to treat relationships between people and God and people and people as primary and ahead of program and work.

Through the years this vision has been in the process of fulfillment. We are not a perfect congregation by any means. We still need a deeper sense of community, of fellowship, of responsibility to one another, of interdependence and of involvement in the world. But we are on the way and God has been faithful in fulfilling this vision as we through the years have lived in the light of it, believing that it would come to pass and doing whatever we are led of God to do to implement it.

This book is not being written in the presumption that here is the only way to think of the church. It is simply one way which has been very satisfying for pastors and people—and we are happy to commend it to others.

THE GOING CHURCH

Come to me, all who labor and are heavy laden, and I will give you rest.

Matthew 11:28

Go therefore and make disciples of all nations, baptizing them in the name of the Father and of the Son and of the Holy Spirit, teaching them to observe all that I have commanded you; and lo, I am with you always to the close of the age.

Matthew 28:19-20

Chapter 2

The Going Church

The Christian life is elliptical; it revolves around two foci—one an invitation and the other a commission. The invitation is that of Jesus Christ, "Come unto Me. . . ." The commission, also from Jesus Christ, is "Go ye into all the world. . . ." The healthy Christian life revolves around the coming and the going.

There are those who are always coming. The sum total of their Christian life and labor is meetings at the church or activities which involve the church work, the church establishment, the church organization. They attend the services morning and evening on Sunday, they generally go to the Sunday school class and if there is a Sunday evening meeting, they attend that. They are faithful at Wednesday night services and they are probably in the choir, on an official board, or in Sunday school work. Their total involvement is in the Christian community with the Christian establishment. That is what they think of as being their service to Jesus Christ.

There is nothing wrong with this as far as it goes. If the religious establishment itself is not maintained, it will not provide the resources needed in the community. But the point is that some people see this as the total context of the Christian experience. In other words, their lives invert around the invitation "come." Their activity is exclusively institutional church-centered.

Then there are the others who are always going. They are disenchanted with the Christian establishment or disillusioned and fed up with it. To them it is irrelevant. They have given up fellowship with other believers and they no longer come to church or other meetings. They are busy going—going about doing good, going out into the community to help the community. This is the sum total of their involvement as Christian servants. Of course, there is nothing wrong with this as far as it goes, but this is only half of the Christian experience and they make it the whole. The total involvement of their Christian life is exclusively going.

Now those who revolve simply around the invitation, who are meeting-centered in their Christian experience, develop a kind of spiritual dyspepsia, a spiritual satiation and stagnancy. On the other hand, those who are always going rarely have anything to offer when they get there. Their intentions are good but they lack spiritual resources to benefit those to whom they go under the duress of their incentive. Just as the healthy body demands a balance between intake and elimination, the healthy Christian needs to come to Christ, to practice fellowship, to join with others in worship and instruction so that he may be nurtured, strengthened and equipped for the purpose of going into the world where the need is. There he is to minister in the name of the Lord Jesus Christ, in the power of the Holy Spirit and in the love of God. That is where the work is— out there in the world.

The healthy Christian experience is a balance of coming and going, of intake and service, of receiving and giving, of nurture and labor.

EXPECTATION AND SATISFACTION

How is it then, brethren? when ye come together, every one of you hath a psalm, hath a doctrine, hath a tongue, hath a revelation, hath an interpretation. Let all things be done unto edifying. If any man speak in an unknown tongue, let it be by two, or at the most by three, and that by course; and let one interpret. But if there be no interpreter, let him keep silence in the church; and let him speak to himself, and to God. Let the prophets speak two or three, and let the other judge. If any thing be revealed to another that sitteth by, let the first hold his peace. For ye may all prophesy one by one, that all may learn, and all may be comforted. And the spirits of the prophets are subject to the prophets. For God is not the author of confusion, but of peace, as in all churches of the saints.

—1 Corinthians 14:26-33 KJV

Chapter 3

Expectation and Satisfaction

Imagine yourself in the Sunday morning service of Fourth Presbyterian Church of Bethesda, Maryland.

Good morning! Greetings in the name of the Lord Jesus Christ, whom we gather to worship as God and Savior. We are here this morning in the confidence that He is in our midst, though invisible, as He promised, "Where two or three are gathered in my name, there am I in their midst." He knows each of us in the total context of our lives. He knows the circumstances from which we come, the future into which we go and our present condition as we are here this morning together. He understands all about us—our sins, our weaknesses, our failures, our hopes, our dreams, our aspirations. He knows our needs better than we know them ourselves and He desires to meet us this morning in some very personal, life-changing way that will help us with those needs and equip us for the work that lies ahead wherever we go, whatever we do. He loves each of us. He desires to make Himself known to us this morning. He wants this to be a fresh experience of reality, of love, of acceptance, of forgiveness for each one of us. There is no reluctance on His part to do this. If there is any reluctance at all, it is on our part.

Therefore, let us open our hearts to this invisible Presence this morning. Let us believe His promise to be in the midst. Let us take off our masks. Let us be wide open to any unexpected meeting between Him and us. It may occur at any moment—during a prayer, the singing of a hymn, the reading of the Scripture or some incidental, little thing that happens in the service. It may come long before the sermon, so do not wait for the sermon to bring the blessing. He may meet you in such a way, with such blessing before the sermon that you will barely hear it because your mind and heart will be preoccupied with an experience which came earlier in the service. Let our expectation be toward Jesus Christ this morning whatever our situation. Let each one of us expect Him to meet us and to help us and to prepare us for the coming week. We will not be disappointed.

It is a great privilege to welcome our visitors

to the service this morning. Thank you for being with us. We trust that you have had no inconvenience in parking and that you are in a comfortable place and that you have already sensed that we receive you in the love and affection of Jesus Christ.

As we gather here this morning, we are not an audience of disconnected individual spectators, waiting to be entertained. We are a community of faith. We are brothers and sisters in Christ—the family of God. We accept you as part of that community. We are members of the body of which Jesus Christ is the head and we trust you are a member of that body. We are a priesthood of believers and have a priestly responsibility to each other and to you, to pray for each other, to encourage each other, to care for each other. We believe that ministry comes not only from the pulpit or from the chancel to the pew, but that ministry should be going on all the time in the midst of the congregation, that each member of the congregation is a minister.

Therefore, let us be open to each other. Let there be no invisible walls separating us. Let us not be afraid of each other. Let us be open to whatever contact the Holy Spirit wants to make between us. Remember that we may not be here for what we are going to receive but for what the Spirit of God wants to give through us. Maybe He seated you where you are because someone near you needs something He wants to give through you this morning. You may not be aware of the need or even aware that you are helping. Maybe it is just a smile or handshake or some warm acknowledgment which to that person means acceptance. If each of us is sensitive to the Holy Spirit and sensitive to those around us this morning, the Holy Spirit will use us as ministers, as priests in each other's lives.

Let us take a moment to pray for each other: Father in heaven, we thank You for the pleasure of each other's company this morning, for the privilege of being here together to worship Jesus Christ. We thank You for His invisible presence, and we pray that we may be very sensitive to His presence and to each other. We thank You that You know our needs. You know where we need forgiveness, You know the one who is lonely, You know the one who is bewildered or perplexed or frustrated, You know the one who is discouraged, You know the one who has financial difficulty or a chronic, nagging illness. You know every need that we bring to this meeting this morning, Lord. Now we pray that You will so minister in us and through us that those needs will be met and that You will use each of us in any way You wish with the others to meet those needs. Grant, O God, that the Holy Spirit will fill us all with the love of Christ so that it overflows us and those about us feel it. Help us to love one another and to demonstrate that we are Your disciples. We pray that each one in the sanctuary, each one in a classroom during this hour, and each one listening on the radio will enjoy a fresh encounter with the living God in Christ which will be life-changing. We pray for the one in front of us, for the one behind, for the one on the left and the one on the right. In Jesus' name. Amen.

What you have just read above is a composite of what is said to the congregation of Fourth Presbyterian Church each Sunday morning at the time called in the bulletin "The Pastoral Greetings." Sometimes the prayer follows the greeting. Other times the prayer is just before the sermon. If there are announcements, they are made following the greeting. This is followed by the "Missions Minute" when some ministry in which the church is interested, or ought to be interested, is presented to the congregation. The "Pastoral Prayer" follows that.

Sometimes, though not always, an opportunity is made for the congregation to make actual physical contact with one another at this time in the service. We may stand and join hands as we sing together "Blest Be the Tie That Binds Our Hearts in Christian Love." We urge everyone to join hands across the center aisle and at the end of each aisle so that the contact is unbroken throughout the whole congregation. Sometimes we take a moment to have the people turn and greet one another in an informal way, "Good morning, it's a pleasure to be beside you. God bless you." Sometimes we do what is called "passing the peace" when the pastor says to his associates, "The peace of God be with you," and the associates on the platform in turn "pass" it to the choir. Two pastors walk down the aisle "passing the peace" to each one sitting on the center aisle who then pass it along their pew. Sometimes this is done at the end of the service. We try to do other things occasionally which will help us to be aware of each other in more than a perfunctory, casual encounter.

Not everyone is happy with this although only a few have been critical. Many have expressed gratitude, not only for the greeting, but for the physical contact as we sing "Blest Be the Tie That Binds" or as there is opportunity to greet one another in the service. Of course, if the people are invited to greet one another in the service, it becomes rather noisy and some who are used to a quiet service find it offensive. A few find it offensive to be asked to make some physical contact like holding hands while singing "Blest Be the Tie That Binds." But those criticisms are few and far between and the great majority of the comments are words of gratitude and hope that we will always do something like this.

The reason we do these things, of course, is that we think this way about the church. We have grown through the years to feel that ministry should be going on all the time in the congre-

gation. This is a change from the early days
when it was felt that the real ministry came when
the sermon was preached and the people waited
to hear the sermon, treating everything else as
preliminary. We have learned that God may meet
a worshiper early in the service in some unexpected way, some incidental, unpredictable way,
that no one would ever expect to bring blessing
from the Lord. It could be a greeting early in the
service as someone lonely enters the sanctuary
and is smiled on by one with a warm and loving countenance. It may be a gentle greeting or
a handshake and this lonely one, for the first time
perhaps in a long time, feels accepted, feels that
he belongs. We do this because we think this way
about the church. We really believe this. We think
that every Sunday morning and Sunday evening should be an experience with the living God
for every worshiper. We believe that God does
know each one in the total context of his life and
if the service is conducted properly in the Holy
Spirit, each worshiper in his own way will have
some kind of encounter with the living God in that
service.

Significantly, the congregation has begun to
think this way and to behave this way. When
people unite with the church, rarely in their
testimony before the elders do they refer to
the preaching or the music. Again and again they
give testimony to the fact that they felt they belonged, they felt acceptance, they felt love in the

midst of the congregation and it was this that drew them to the church. So in general the congregation has grown into this way of fellowship when gathered. I'm sure there are those who resist all these efforts to personalize the Sunday morning service and perhaps some have left because they did not like this informality. They might even think of it as emotionalism.

The important thing is that the congregation has come to the place where strangers are welcome however they are dressed, no matter how they look, whatever the color of their skin, from wherever they come. For the most part, with few exceptions, visitors feel welcome in the service. As the pastor has thought this way about the church and expressed it in the service, the people have come to think this way and to act this way. It is a loving congregation and I can say for myself as pastor that every service is an experience of forgiveness, acceptance, affirmation and love.

COMMUNITY

...let us consider how to stir up one another to love and good works, not neglecting to meet together, as is the habit of some, but encouraging one another....
Hebrews 10:24-25

Chapter 4

Community

Think of the church as community.

Alienation is not only the deepest problem of the last third of the twentieth century, it is the deepest problem in history. Alienation began with man's self-alienation from God, the consequences of which are man's alienation from his fellow-man, whether in families or as friends, colleagues, peers, races, nations, etc. War is the inescapable result of man's self-alienation from God.

Sin is that which separates or alienates man from God and man from man. It is this which Christ entered history to resolve. In his second letter to the Corinthians, chapter 5, the Apostle Paul declares that God has committed to us, who have been born again in Christ, the ministry and the message of reconciliation, to wit that, "God was in Christ reconciling the world unto Himself." The heart of the Christian message is reconciliation. The heart of the Christian experience ought to be reconciliation. Whatever else the church demonstrates to the world it should demonstrate reconciliation.

Jesus said to His disciples on the eve of His betrayal, "A new commandment I give that you love one another as I have loved you, that you also love one another. By this all men will know that you are my disciples if you have love for one another" (John 13:34, 35). If love is proof to the world of our discipleship, it can be inferred that one reason the world does not recognize us as His disciples is that it simply does not see any demonstration of love among us. Our failure to love one another leaves the world without evidence that we are His disciples.

In His high priestly prayer, Jesus prayed, "that they may all be one; even as thou, Father, art in me, and I in thee, that they may also be one in us, so that the world may believe that thou hast sent me. . . . that they may be one even as we are one, I in them and thou in me, that they may become perfectly one so that the world may know that thou hast sent me and hast loved them even as thou hast loved me" (John 17:21-23). Indisputably, the evidence to the world that the Father sent the Son and loves the world as He loves the Son is the fact that His disciples are united. It follows that disunited or divided disciples do not witness that the Son has been sent by the Father or that the Father loves the world as He loved the Son.

If we do not love one another, if we are not united, all of our protestations and professions to the contrary notwithstanding, the world will not see us as disciples of Jesus Christ; the world will not believe that the Father sent the Son or that He loves them as He loved the Son. One of the observations the world made of the church during the time of the apostolic fathers was, "Lo, how they love one another." At the end of Acts 2, following a beautiful description of the togetherness of the apostolic church, Dr. Luke records concerning them that they were "praising God and having favor with all the people." What is the explanation for the favor which the church had with all the people?

Three things happened at Pentecost, each one fundamental to the mission of the church in the world. First, every believer was filled with the Holy Spirit. Dr. Luke records that when the Spirit of God came at Pentecost, tongues of fire lighted on each of the disciples and they were filled with the Holy Spirit and each one "spoke as the Spirit gave him utterance." It is clear from this that when the church is what she ought to be, i.e., when she is in health—in spiritual health —every believer is filled with the Holy Spirit and every believer speaks as the Spirit gives him utterance in witnessing to the love of God in Christ. This ought to be the desire of every pastor

—that every member of his congregation be filled with the Holy Spirit and that every member of his congregation be led to speak of the reconciling love of God in Christ whenever and wherever the Spirit directs. This is evangelism by the whole church. The Gospel of Jesus Christ is proclaimed by every member. Wherever the church is in the person of each disciple, there the Gospel of Christ is being talked about as the Spirit of God gives each disciple utterance.

There were those who questioned this phenomenon at Pentecost and the record declares that Peter stood up to answer the critics and in so doing preached his Pentecostal sermon. This is the second fact of Pentecost—proclamation. Peter preached. This is certainly a basic part of the fundamental strategy of the church in the world—proclamation. When God gave the pulpit centrality in the Reformation, He brought the church back to the proclamation. God has never repudiated or abrogated this ministry in the church. It is as important today as it was at Pentecost and in any age of the church since. Proclamation is still at the heart of Christian worship and it ought to be the desire of every pastor that his pulpit be strong in its exposition of the Word of God.

Preaching has recently come under severe criticism as being irrelevant and archaic. But the problem has not been preaching as such but the kind of preaching which has brought proclamation into disrepute. Expository preaching has never been irrelevant—it is when the exposition of Scripture is abandoned and the sacred desk is used for political diatribes and sociological essays that preaching has failed.

A third thing occurred at Pentecost and it became the matrix of everything else that happened in Acts and has happened of eternal significance in the church since Pentecost—the Christian community was born. On that day by the supernatural power of the Holy Spirit, those 120 individual disciples were galvanized into one, inseparable, indivisible, indestructible living organism—the body of which Christ is the head. They literally became members one of another, needing one another, responsible to one another as the members of a physical body are responsible and necessary to each other. The delicate, sensitive, harmonious relationship that the Spirit of God produced in these disciples is described beautifully in Paul's first letter to the Corinthians, chapter 12.

What that first century world saw was the phenomenon of people of all walks of life loving one another, serving one another, caring for one another, praying for one another. Slaves and free men were in that community. Rich and poor were in that fellowship. Roman citizens and non-Roman citizens were in that community. Members of the establishment and those violently opposed to the establishment were part of that community.

The intelligentsia and the illiterate were members of that community. To the utter amazement of the world outside, they were bound together in an unexplainable love and unity.

Think of the culture into which that little New Testament community was born. It was a violent, brutal, hostile, immoral culture. The majority of the population were slaves. The cultured citizens of the Roman empire passed their leisure sitting in amphitheaters howling with delight as lions destroyed human life or as human beings killed one another in the arena below. One historian writing of those days in Rome said that any citizen of Rome who could invent a more brutal way to destroy human life was guaranteed a place of honor and high prestige in the empire. Life was cheap. A man could kill his slave if he was unhappy with some little bit of service which the slave performed. Parents could abandon a baby in the gutter or the garbage if the birth was unwanted. Violence and hostility were everywhere. The population was hopelessly fragmentized but in the midst of all this unrelieved alienation was born a new, unprecedented organism— a community of love, a little microcosm of the Roman Empire bound together in the love of Jesus Christ. Is it any wonder that the New Testament community had the impact on the world that it did? Do you wonder that they were known as "those who turned the world upside down"? Do you see why the world listened when they talked, when they witnessed of the love they found in Jesus Christ? Is it any wonder that the church grew as rapidly as it did in those early days despite persecution, despite everything that could be done to prevent its growth? By the very quality of its life together that New Testament church demonstrated to the world what it meant by what it preached when it said, "God was in Christ reconciling the world to Himself and therefore besought the world, be ye reconciled unto God."

In Acts 2:44-47 Luke describes this community in these words: ". . . all who believed were together and had all things in common; and they sold their possessions and goods and distributed them to all as any had need. And day by day attending the temple together and breaking bread in their homes, they partook of food with glad and generous hearts praising God and having favor with all the people." In Acts 4:32-34, Luke describes that New Testament community in this way: "Now the company of those who believed were of one heart and soul and no one said that any of the things which he possessed was his own but they had everything in common. There was not a needy person among them for as many as were possessors of lands or houses sold them and brought the proceeds of what was sold and laid them at the apostles' feet and distribution was made to each as any had need."

It is clear in the narrative which follows in

Acts 5 that this common life was a voluntary one, that no one was required to sell his possessions and lay them at the apostles' feet, that this common life was not legislated. It is also clear that this did not always work, that sin and selfishness emerged early in the community and severe judgment had to fall on two of its members, i.e., Ananias and his wife, Sapphira. But the important thing is this, that when the Holy Spirit came upon those 120 disciples and then 3,000 who were baptized on the day of Pentecost, they were together and had all things in common, and they formed in the power of the Holy Spirit one living, loving, caring community which was an absolutely unique phenomenon, a miracle in a violent, hostile, immoral world.

The exquisite relationships sovereignly arranged by God in that community are described by the Apostle Paul in First Corinthians 12:13-26. So delicate was this arrangement that, "... If one member suffers, all suffer together; if one member is honored, all rejoice together" (v. 26). So unlike that New Testament community is the contemporary church that the opposite condition not uncommonly prevails. When a member is honored, other members suffer and when one suffers others rejoice. Why do we not weep over this hardness, this selfishness, this unlove in our present day congregations? Why do we not treat as intolerable such conditions and give ourselves to their remedy? Why do we not consider com-

munity as the priority for the ministry and deal
with it as fundamental to outreach?

John, writing his first epistle, took these relationships seriously. Writing to his "children"
in the faith, the beloved apostle said that his
purpose in declaring the life which had been
manifested was that they might have fellowship
one with another, a fellowship which was "with
the Father and with His Son, Jesus Christ" (1:3).
The key to this fellowship was confession and
forgiveness.

> This is the message we have heard from him
> and proclaim to you, that God is light and
> in him is no darkness at all. If we say we
> have fellowship with him while we walk in
> darkness, we lie and do not live according
> to the truth; but if we walk in the light, as
> he is in the light, we have fellowship with
> one another, and the blood of Jesus his Son
> cleanses us from all sin. If we say we have
> no sin, we deceive ourselves, and the truth is
> not in us. If we confess our sins, he is faith-
> ful and just, and will forgive our sins and
> cleanse us from all unrighteousness. If we
> say we have not sinned, we make him a
> liar, and his word is not in us. (1 John 1:5-10)

Characteristic of this fellowship is love for
one another, a truth admonished throughout the
epistle. John's pastor heart longed for this relationship. With profound eloquence he urged his
readers to walk in this light. We who shepherd
the people of God ought to heed this dominant
concern of the apostle and give to it the priority

45

it demands. Perhaps less time on recruiting, programming, training and mobilizing for outreach and more time on leading the people in fellowship would issue in spontaneous, fruitful mission.

James, too, the practical one, must have felt the urgency of the interpersonal relationships within the community as he exhorted, "Therefore, confess your sins one to another . . . that you may be healed" (James 5:16).

Certainly Jesus gave priority to fellowship. Following His giving of the model prayer, He warned, "For if you forgive men their trespasses, your heavenly Father also will forgive you; but if you do not forgive men their trespasses, neither will your Father forgive your trespasses" (Matthew 6:14-15). To Him reconciliation between brothers had priority over the offering of gifts. "So if you are offering your gift at the altar, and there remember that your brother has something against you, leave your gift there before the altar and go; first be reconciled to your brother and then come and offer your gift" (Matthew 5:23-24).

Paul, concerned for the unity of believers, exhorted them "endeavoring to keep the unity of the Spirit in the bond of peace" (Ephesians 4:3). He testified that the passion of his life was to bring everyone to his "full maturity in Christ," an objective which he pursued "with all the energy God gives me" (Colossians 1:27-28). To him maturity was not so much an individual matter as it was corporate (Ephesians 4:13-16).

No less exquisite is God's provision for the nurture and growth of the relationships in the community.

> Now concerning spiritual gifts, brethren, I do not want you to be uninformed. You know that when you were heathen, you were led astray to dumb idols, however you may have been moved. Therefore I want you to understand that no one speaking by the Spirit of God ever says "Jesus be cursed!" and no one can say "Jesus is Lord" except by the Holy Spirit. Now there are varieties of gifts, but the same Spirit; and there are varieties of service, but the same Lord; and there are varieties of working, but it is the same God who inspires them all in every one. To each is given the manifestation of the Spirit for the common good. To one is given through the Spirit the utterance of wisdom, and to another the utterance of knowledge according to the same Spirit, to another faith by the same Spirit, to another gifts of healing by the one Spirit, to another the working of miracles, to another prophecy, to another the ability to distinguish between spirits, to another various kinds of tongues, to another the interpretation of tongues. All these are inspired by one and the same Spirit, who apportions to each one individually as he wills. For just as the body is one and has many members, and all the members of the body, though many, are one body, so it is with Christ.   (1 Corinthians 12:1-12)

When the Holy Spirit was given at Pentecost, He distributed to the members of the body vari-

47

ous gifts, complementing one another and fulfilling the whole. This "manifestation of the Spirit" was given to every disciple that each should be essentially involved in the health and maturation of all (v. 7). The gifts were not given that the individual believer might use them at his discretion; they were to be managed by the Lord Himself (v. 4) as they were energized by the Father (v. 6). As the human body is coordinated by the head so the gifts are to be governed by the Head of the church, the Lord Jesus Christ.

The fellowship of believers is the order of first importance to the pastor. Think community!

FELLOWSHIP

Now the company of those who believed were of one heart and soul, and no one said that any of the things which he possessed was his own, but they had everything in common.

(Acts 4:32)

Chapter 5

Fellowship

One of the conditions in the New Testament community which resulted in spontaneous propagation of the Gospel is described in Acts 2:42. There Luke reports, "And they devoted themselves to the apostles' teaching and fellowship, to the breaking of bread, and the prayers." The Apostolic Church had a four-fold program: apostolic doctrine, fellowship, breaking of bread, and prayer. There is nothing in the passage to indicate that fellowship was any less important than, for example, the apostles' doctrine or prayer or the breaking of bread, which could have meant either communion itself or the agape feast. Apparently in the Apostolic Church fellowship was as important as doctrine and prayer and sacrament. Those New Testament Christians took the teaching of the apostles seriously, they took the sacrament of the Lord's supper seriously, they took prayer seriously, and they took fellowship seriously. The sad and contradictory fact is that in many of the churches today where doctrine and prayer, if not the sacraments, are taken most seriously and where there seems to be the most zealous concern for evangelism and outreach and mission, fellowship is ignored and/or neglected as though unimportant.

To the Apostle John, the fellowship was the supreme motivation for evangelism. He wrote in his first letter, chapter one, verse three: "That which we have seen and heard declare we unto you that you may have fellowship with us and our fellowship is with the Father and with His Son, Jesus Christ." He adds in verse four that the joy of this fellowship is increased when the fellowship is extended, then continues in the balance of the chapter to describe how fellowship can be maintained and what disrupts fellowship. So far as the Apostle John was concerned, fellowship was not a means to an end but an end in itself. This in fact is why God created man, for fellowship with Himself. It is this fundamental relationship which was broken, alienating and separating man from his Creator; and it is this sin which Jesus Christ came into the world to remedy by the process of reconciliation through His redemption on the cross. Hence, fellowship is not simply a peripheral and incidental luxury in the church of Christ; it is a central necessity.

It is, in fact, the ultimate reality which God purposes in His sovereign will to achieve as the consummation of His redemptive plan.

On the eve of His betrayal, arrest, conviction and crucifixion, our Lord prayed for His disciples (John 17). That brief prayer centered in one petition, "... that they may be one, as Thou Father art in Me and I in Thee ..." (verses 20 and 22, caps mine).

Our Lord's profoundest "death wish," as it were, was the unity of His disciples. One can think of many other concerns He might have expressed in that exquisitely significant situation, nevertheless His preoccupation was that those who believed on Him might be one. The desire of our Lord is not strange, however, when we consider the model of the unity for which He prayed—"... as Thou Father art in Me and I in Thee." His dominant longing as He faced His ultimate humiliation was that the disciples might enjoy the fellowship which He and the Father enjoyed in the Godhead.

Before Creation, when all there was was God, the Father, Son and Holy Spirit were united in an eternal, harmonious fellowship of love. Here was perfect unity, perfect peace, reality in the consummate. The first act of creation after man was woman. "God saw it was not good for man to be alone, so He made woman—and brought her to the man—and the man said, 'She shall be bone of my bone and flesh of my flesh.' " Therefore, the author of Genesis concludes, "A man shall leave his father and mother and cleave unto his wife, and they two shall be one flesh." In the beautiful unity of the man and his wife, God was demonstrating that relationship which He longed to enjoy with the crowning glory of His creation, man. This first union was the basic and essential foundation of the social order and history vividly confirms the fact that no civilization can long withstand its disintegration. When marriage and the home collapse, the entire social structure inevitably follows.

Writing millenniums later, the Apostle Paul draws from Genesis the unforgettable lesson that the relationship between husband and wife is the supreme human relationship analagous to that which God desires with His creatures, preeminently manifest in the relationship between Christ and His church (Ephesians 5:22-31). This is what history is all about. This is the divine plan and purpose, as stated so triumphantly by Paul in Ephesians 1:9 and 10: "Having made known unto us the mystery of his will, according to his good pleasure which he hath purposed in himself: That in the dispensation of the fullness of times he might gather together in one all things in Christ, both which are in heaven, and which are on earth; even in him."

Out of such fellowship flows authentic evangelism, mission, outreach. Fellowship is the matrix of mission.

It is plain, therefore, that no congregation or community of faith can be what it ought to be until it takes fellowship seriously—until it continues steadfastly in fellowship as well as the apostle's doctrine, breaking of bread and prayer. Our Lord's constant concern for this, as mentioned earlier, is expressed in the Sermon on the Mount as He taught the "Lord's Prayer." When He finished that model prayer, He lifted out of it one petition as if to say this is essential to the rest. In effect, that petition was, "If you forgive those who trespass against you so will your father forgive you, if you forgive not those who trespass against you, neither will your Father in heaven forgive you" (Matthew 6:14,15). Likewise, "If you bring your gift to the altar and there remember that any man hath aught against you, leave your gift at the altar, first be reconciled and then come and offer your gift" (Matthew 5:23). In these two instances in the Sermon on the Mount, our Lord made it clear that fellowship was fundamental to life. The unity of brother with brother, believer with believer, disciple with disciple was primary and should be given priority in the life of a church. In other words, anything that destroys or disrupts or minimizes fellowship should be treated as intolerable in the life of the community.

Paul certainly understood this when he declared his passion and purpose in Colossians 1: 27-28, "To whom God would make known what is the riches of the glory of this mystery among the Gentiles which is Christ in you, the hope of glory: Whom we preach, warning every man, and teaching every man in all wisdom; that we may present every man perfect in Christ Jesus." The question is, what is in the mind of the Apostle Paul as he speaks of bringing men to their "full maturity in Christ"? What did Paul understand as maturity?

Not uncommonly among those who are most zealously evangelical, maturity is thought of as a personal, individual matter. One's growth in grace is a private affair, dependent upon the conditions which make for growth, without regard for the maturation of others. Such an attitude produces the "superior" Christian—who compares his own spirituality with others, competes with those who seem to be ahead of him, and prides himself in the fact that he has developed more spiritually (whatever he means by that) than others. He actually feels satisfaction when he discovers those who are by his criteria, whatever it is, less spiritual than he.

Nothing could be further from Paul's mind than this when he spoke of maturity. One reference will suffice: "... until we all attain to the unity of the faith and of the knowledge of the Son of God, to mature manhood, to the measure of the stature of the fulness of Christ; so that we may no longer be children, tossed to and fro and carried about with every wind of doctrine, by the cunning of men, by their craftiness in deceitful wiles. Rather, speaking the truth in love, we are to grow every way into him who is the head, into Christ, from whom the whole body, joined and knit together by every joint with which it is supplied, when each part is working properly, makes bodily growth and upbuilds itself in love" (Ephesians 4:13-16). To Paul all believers were members of a single organism of which Christ was the head. As members of a single body, they must grow together, each part interdependent with all the other parts. It is a tragedy when all parts of the human body do not grow simultaneously. When one grows more slowly than the rest or one grows excessively, the whole body is affected seriously. So it is with the body of Christ so beautifully described by Paul in First Corinthians 12. No member of the body can get along without the others and all are indispensable to the body. True maturity is realized when all grow together in their relationship with Christ, the Head, and with one another. Fellowship is central to spiritual maturation and love is the supreme evidence of the mature, Spirit-filled and Spirit-led disciple.

Two of the most remarkable promises Christ made are recorded in Matthew 18:19-20. Actually they are one promise with its condition: "If two of you shall agree as touching anything on earth they shall ask, it shall be done for them of my Father which is in heaven." (the promise) "For wherever two or three are gathered together in my name, there am I in the midst of them" (the condition).

That incredible promise, which we find impossible to take seriously because it is so categorical, is at the heart of our Lord's very practical discussion of forgiveness and reconciliation in the community (Matthew 18:1-8; 21-35). Fellowship is crucial to the promise.

> Beloved, let us love one another; for love is of God, and he who loves is born of God and knows God. He who does not love does not know God; for God is love. In this the love of God was made manifest among us, that God sent his only Son into the world, so that we might live through him. In this is love, not that we loved God but that he loved us and sent his Son to be the expiation for our sins. Beloved, if God so loved us, we also ought to love one another. No man has ever seen God; if we love one another, God abides in us and his love is perfected in us. By this we know that we abide in him and he in us, because he has given us of his own Spirit. And we have seen and testify that the Father has sent his Son as the Savior of the world. Whoever confesses that Jesus is the Son of God, God abides in him, and he in God. So we know and believe the love God has for us. God is love, and he who abides in love abides in God, and God abides in him. In this is love perfected with us, that we may have confidence for the day of judgment, because as he is so are we in this world. There is no fear in love, but perfect love casts out fear. For fear has to do with

punishment, and he who fears is not per-
fected in love. We love, because he first
loved us. If any one says, "I love God," and
hates his brother, he is a liar; for he who
does not love his brother whom he has seen,
cannot love God whom he has not seen.
(1 John 4:7-20)

MATRIX OF MISSION

We repeat, we really saw and heard what we are now writing to you about. We want you to be with us in this—in this fellowship with God the Father, and Jesus Christ his Son. We must write and tell you about it, because the more that fellowship extends, the greater the joy it brings to us who are already in it.

(1 John 1:3-4 Phillips)

Chapter 6

Matrix of Mission

If one were to begin from scratch to build a theology of evangelism and mission on the basis of what he found in the New Testament epistles, he would probably be impressed with the paucity of material upon which to build. For example, he would not find the apostles reminding their readers of the Great Commission. He would not find a systems approach to evangelism or mission. Nor would he find the Apostle Paul issuing extensive instructions to those to whom he wrote as to how to win people to Christ. He would not find evangelistic quotas and goals and slogans to promote them.

This is not to argue from silence that the apostles never reminded their disciples or readers of the Great Commission and the obligation of each disciple to be a witness for Jesus Christ. Certainly Paul felt his universal obligation as a witness for Christ (Romans 1:14). But it is to say that the weight of the exhortation and instruction in the epistles has to do with the relationship of believer with believer in the community, in the body of Christ. The implication can be clearly drawn that when these relationships are right, i.e., when the brothers and sisters love one another and when they are abiding in Christ, evangelism and mission will be the normal and healthy result of such relationships.

The last sentence in the second chapter of Acts illustrates this point. There Luke attaches to his description of that New Testament community, this statement, "And the Lord added to their number day by day those who were being saved." In other words, when all who believed were together and had all things in common—when they were selfless in their attitude toward their possessions—when they worshiped together daily and broke bread in their homes—when they partook of food with glad and generous hearts—when they praised God, they had favor with all the people as a result of which evangelism happened. It was inevitable: "The Lord added to the church day by day those that were being saved" (Acts 2:47).

Other references in Acts bear out this fact. Chapter 6, verse 7, for example, "And the word of God increased and the number of the disciples multiplied greatly in Jerusalem, and a great many of the priests were obedient to the faith." When the word of God increased, evangelism happened, the number of the disciples increased greatly in Jerusalem. The multiplication of disciples was the normal result of the ministry of the Word in the city. In Acts 9:31 Luke records, "So the church throughout all Judea, and Galilee and Samaria had peace and was built up; and walking in the fear of the Lord and in the comfort of the Holy Spirit, it was multiplied." Here again, multiplication is the result of conducive conditions in the community. The church had peace, she was built up, she walked in the fear of the Lord and in the comfort of the Holy Spirit, as a result of which, she was multiplied. So in Acts 16:5, where it is recorded, "So the churches were strengthened in the faith and they increased in numbers daily." The condition was the strengthening of the churches; the effect or result was daily increase in numbers. In these references one is conscious of a spontaneous explosion which resulted when conditions in the body were right for such an explosion or expansion. The emphasis was not on the expansion; the emphasis was upon the conditions which allowed the expansion to take place.

Here one does not find the churches organizing to reach the world with the Gospel of Jesus Christ. But what one does find is the Gospel being scattered widely and rapidly because the church is in such a healthy condition that this can happen.

These New Testament Christians were not less human, less weak and sinful than our modern generation. They did not have some unusual advantage which we do not have in our generation. As a matter of fact, they had few of the advantages which we now enjoy by which to spread the Gospel of Jesus Christ. They had none of the modern technology which is available to us as well as the knowledge and experience in communication which we know today. Yet because of the relationship to Christ and to each other to which they devoted themselves, the Gospel spread through them everywhere throughout the world and the number of the disciples increased daily.

A cursory reading of the epistles of the New Testament will readily indicate in those sections which deal with man's response to God and with man's responsibility to his fellow man this truth: those people were heavily weighted with the burden of the responsibility of brother to Christian brother, to the relationships within the family of Christ, within the body, within the community.

The church is failing in evangelism and mission today not because she does not know what she ought to do or even how to do it, not because she does not have the tools for such a worldwide propagation of the Gospel of Jesus Christ—but because there is no incentive. And there is no incentive because the conditions in the body which produce that incentive are absent. You cannot legislate evangelism and mission. No amount of organizing and planning, programming, training and exhorting will replace the spontaneous expansion of the church when the Spirit of God reigns in the hearts of believers and they are in fellowship with one another as well as with the Father and with His Son, Jesus Christ.

THE WORK OF THE CHURCH

I therefore, the prisoner of the Lord, beseech you that ye walk worthy of the vocation wherewith ye are called. . . . But unto every one of us is given grace according to the measure of the gift of Christ.

(Ephesians 4:1, 7)

Chapter 7

The Work of the Church

How does one think about the church so far as
the membership of the church is concerned? How
does one look at the congregation, the people who
are on the rolls of the church? Does he see them
as men and women to be mobilized to help him
with his ministry? This seems to be the common
view, the conventional way of thinking about the
congregation. The minister is a professional or-
ganizer and programmer. His task is to mobilize
the members of the congregation to fulfill the
ministry which he has been given in that situation. This way of thinking about the members of
the church can lead to deep frustration on the
part of pastors and as a matter of fact, has, in
some cases, destroyed them. Frustrated by the
immense task of mobilizing his people for ministry, he has settled for just thinking up tasks to

keep them busy. Such thinking is not helped by members of the congregation who, before or after they unite with the church, ask the question, "Do you have a job for me?" or "What can I do for the church?" The minister finds himself preoccupied with the employment of the people in church work—at times inventing tasks to keep them interested and busy. When you reflect on this you realize it is impossible to keep the members of the church busy in church work because what needs doing for the organization, the establishment, the building and the program of the church requires relatively few of the members.

This was resolved for me when one of the busiest, most effective members of the Hollywood First Presbyterian Church approached me one day. He asked what I thought about the possibility of his becoming president of his local school board. He said that should he accept this position, it would mean he would have to drop out of many of the activities of the church because the responsibilities in the new position would keep him tied down pretty much, not only because of the meetings and business at hand but also because of the social life that would be involved. He would pretty much have to withdraw from much that he was doing in the Hollywood Church. Although he would be able to attend Sunday morning and perhaps occasionally Sunday evening, he would have to withdraw from the official board. He would be unable to be active in the young marrieds' class in which he had been so involved for so long. In short, he would be taken pretty much from the life of the congregation except for Sunday worship. My reaction to this was resentment that a "secular" organization would steal such a devoted young man from the activities of the church. However, as I prayed about it, it occurred to me that nothing could be finer than that a committed Christian such as he serve as president of a local school board. Think what it would mean if every school board in the United States would have as its president a truly dedicated Christian!

I learned several significant lessons in this experience. One, I learned the importance of the dispersion of the people of God, about which I will speak in a later chapter. Second, I began to realize there is a real distinction between church work and the work of the church. As I pondered the loss of this fine young man from the congregation, I asked the question, "How many do we need to really do the work of the organization of this church?" Supposing each person could have only one task, no "double duty" so to speak, what would the personnel requirement be? As a matter of fact, many of the men and women in the church had several jobs, not only singing in the choir but teaching Sunday school—not only serving on the official boards but ushering. They were very busy with the ecclesiastical establishment. But suppose that each could hold only one job,

73

how many would it take to do the work of that large congregation? At the time, the membership was about 7,000. To my amazement I found that it would require only 365 to do the work that was required to maintain the program of the First Presbyterian Church of Hollywood—only 365 for choirs, teaching and administering Sunday school, official boards, the various organizations of the church, etc. This meant that most of the members of the church could never have a job in the institution. It followed, therefore, that if the work of the church is what is done for the institution, very few, relatively speaking, will ever have an opportunity to do the work of the church. Imagine, therefore, the plight of the pastor who begins to feel that he has to find a task for every member of the church. No wonder some leave the ministry.

It became apparent that the work of the church is not what is done for the institution, the organization, the establishment. The real work of the church is what is done between Sundays when the church is scattered all over the metropolitan area where it is located—in homes, in schools, in offices, on construction jobs, in market places. This is the work of the church and it requires every single member. The responsibility of the pastor is to equip every member to do the work of the church wherever he is between Sundays. This radically alters the pastor's way of thinking about his responsibility to the congregation. No longer do they represent men and women who are to be mobilized to do the work of his ministry; but on the contrary, they have a ministry wherever they are and God has called the pastor to equip them for their ministry. This is the pattern as Paul describes the work of the ministry in the fourth chapter of Ephesians where he begins by reminding the reader that every Christian has a holy vocation which God has given. When Christ "ascended on high and led captivity captive, he gave gifts to men" among which were some apostles, some prophets, some evangelists, some pastors and teachers. The purpose for these gifts to the church was that they should equip the congregation for the work of ministry. Put another way, apostles, prophets, evangelists, pastors and teachers have been mobilized by God to help the members of the community fulfill their ministry wherever they are during the week.

One of the reasons the institutional church has become irrelevant to the extent that it has in our contemporary life is that many Christians have become so busy in church work they have not had time to do the work of the church. The religious establishment, the institution, the organization, the program demanded so much of their time they were not able to be the witness, the minister, the servant of God and man that they were intended to be. Christ intended that they minister where they spend most of their time—in the home, on the campus, on the job, in their social set. They were so involved in church work, they were unable to be involved in the life of the larger community. The establishment preoccupied and preempted them. It is almost as if the church exists for itself, i.e. the church institution. Almost as if the important thing is the building and the program rather than the outreach into the world for which Christ died and to which God sent His church.

The view persists that the serious Christian, the one truly committed, will be active in the life of the religious institution. If he loves Christ he ought to be doing "something for the church." The program of the establishment is equated with service for Christ. As one does this he is "spiritual." In everything else, except as he may sporadically talk to someone in an effort to win him to Christ or get him into the church, he is "secular."

The truth is, everything we do in the church organization, in the church building, in the church program ought to contribute to the church's effectiveness when it is not involved in the building or the program or the organization—when it is out in the world. What happens when the church is gathered, what the official boards do, what the choir does, what the ushers do, what the Sunday school teachers and officers do, ought to be designed to equip every member to fulfill his ministry wherever he is between Sundays. In other words, the measure of the effectiveness of a congregation is not what one sees when the congregation is gathered, not the size of the building, nor the size of the budget, nor the size of the congregation or the Sunday school. The real measure of the effectiveness of a congregation is what happens when the congregation is not in the sanctuary or the Sunday school or meeting officially as boards or committees or councils. The measure of the effectiveness of any local congregation when it is gathered, is the measure of what that congregation is doing when it is dispersed. To put it another way, it is not what the congregation does when it is visible as a congregation that is the criterion for the effectivness of that congregation, but it is what the congregation is doing when it is invisible as a congregation that is the criterion for the effectiveness of that congregation. We will have more to say about this later.

One of the ironic facts about the institutional church is that all of the criteria for its success are materialistic. The pastor is successful or unsuccessful, a local congregation is successful or unsuccessful in terms of dollars and cents, in terms of the size of the plant, in terms of the number of the congregation on the rolls of the church or Sunday morning attendance. The larger the congregation, the building and the budget, the more successful the pastor. This is blandly assumed.

It is not difficult to see that such an attitude about the church leads inevitably to a materialistic attitude and inclines the church inward to itself, making it an introverted or self-centered organization, instead of turning it outward toward the world for which Christ died and into which Christ sends His church. This is the way of love.

It even makes the motivation for evangelism in the local church suspect because it is difficult to separate the desire to get members in the church and build up the congregation from the desire just to see people born again into the Kingdom of God whether they become members of a particular congregation or not.

It can also lead to a false idea of church growth. The local pastor can begin to think he is reaching the world for Christ when all he is doing is drawing Christians from other congregations to his congregation. It is not "adding to the church daily them that are being saved." All that is happening is that those who are already saved (if they are) are moving from one congregation to another and the sum total of those being brought into the Kingdom of God is not increasing at all.

It is quite possible for a congregation, on the basis which seems so acceptable in the contemporary church, to congratulate itself falsely on its growth in numbers and the buildings required to accommodate those numbers. And to praise itself on the budget increase which would normally

78

result from the increase in numbers. Thus a church could consider itself a success evangelistically, when in reality, little evangelism is happening.

EARLY FRUSTRATIONS

And he appointed twelve, to be with him, and to be sent out to preach...."
(Mark 3:14)

Chapter 8

Early Frustrations

My first pastorate was a small Presbyterian church in Coalinga, California, located in the San Joaquin Valley in the central part of the state. Previous to that I had served two terms as the managing director of the Forest Home Christian Conference Center in Southern California and a year and a half as an assistant to the man who had led me to Christ in the Lynwood Presbyterian Church in Kansas City, Missouri.

The little church to which I was called in Coalinga was a thriving church. The pastors before me had been effective in their ministries. I inherited an ideal situation. Most of the officers were committed Christians, the Sunday morning and evening services were well attended, there was a large group of teenage young people, the benevolence budget was unusually high for the size of the congregation, and there were simply no serious problems in the church.

For the first year and a half my ministry there was a very happy one. As I went along with the momentum, God blessed and the church grew. We saw many young people commit themselves to full-time Christian vocations. But as I became better acquainted in the community outside the church I began to realize that relatively speaking our community was unreached for Jesus Christ. It was a proud, prosperous little city. For the most part, the people were good people—conservative, respectable and moral. I can remember, for example, how they boasted that they could go away for a whole summer on vacation and never lock the door of the house. Or they could leave the car on the street overnight with the keys in it without fear of it being stolen. Coalinga was isolated from other cities and pretty much insulated against many of the problems outside. Generally, the people in the community seemed to be getting along quite well without the church. There were fourteen churches in that town of approximately 6,000 people. I began to feel that there was no way for the church to grow in that community——that there were simply no needs there.

One morning at a monthly breakfast I asked our ministerial group to estimate the number of people all of the churches in the community were reaching. I was shocked when we estimated that we were reaching only a little less than ten percent. Most of the leaders in that community were among those who were not involved in the life of any of the churches. I began to feel that the church was way outside the mainstream of life, that important public decisions were being made without any instruction from the Word of God or from the church as such, that the community was running well without spiritual insights and nurture. This led to a feeling of uselessness, as though clergy were important only as maintenance men for an ecclesiastical organization. It seemed as if we were spinning around in a little eddy unattached to the mainstream of life. I began to feel unnecessary as a pastor and longed to do something that people needed.

As I prayed about this it was as if God said to me, "Why are you so sure that this community is getting along without the church—without the Word—without Me? What have you done to find out about this?" This led me to begin what I now call the ministry of listening. I devoted several days a week simply to moving from office to office, shop to shop and out on the oil leases and large farms which surround the city— just being visible and available. Men became used to my presence where they were putting in their daily work and I was soon able to visit with them on their jobs. In a matter of weeks nearly everyone I talked to revealed some sort of need in his life or in the community which, with my orientation, I knew only Jesus Christ could meet.

Then came the next step, how does one communicate Jesus Christ to those people outside the church? How does one help them to see their need and then show them that Christ can meet that need? One book, which had a great influence on my life, given me shortly after my conversion to Christ, was *Every Member Evangelism* by Conant. Long before I entered the pastorate, therefore, I understood that the work of the ministry belonged to the members of the church, not simply to the professional evangelist or pastor, and that the task of the pastor or evangelist was to equip all the members of the church for the work of ministry. I understood that if a community were to be reached for Jesus Christ that community could best be reached when every member of the congregation of the local church was an evangelist, a witness wherever he was during the week. The only trouble with this, as I reflect now upon my thinking in those days, is that I assumed that everyone led to Christ by members of my congregation or everyone I led to Christ would naturally become members of the church which I pastored. We would grow and meet the criteria for the successful church.

Now there were two pressures on me as a pastor. One was the pressure of the organization—the pressure of increasing the membership of the church, increasing the budget (especially the benevolence budget) and, though subconsciously, looking forward to the day when we would require a bigger building to house the growing congregation. The other pressure was external or outreach. Here was a community that needed Christ. The way to reach that community was through the local congregation as the pastor equipped them for this mission. Although I was not particularly aware of it at the time, subsequent experience made me realize that my attitude was crassly commercial. The real pressure was building the institution. After all, this was the way to "succeed" as a pastor. So the outreach was to enlarge the institution. It was impossible to escape this pressure because this was my way of thinking about the church and it was the conventional way and quite acceptable.

I think I was genuinely concerned for the salvation of men in those days. However, that concern was subordinate to the building of the institution. Though I did not realize it then I had a "hidden agenda"—an unverbalized goal or purpose which I was bound to communicate to those I was attempting to reach. And it must also have diluted the congregation's incentive for outreach. At any rate, the congregation did not move as I thought it should and my pressure upon them increased. I still labored under the illusion that my motive was mission but hindsight makes it embarrassingly clear that my primary goal was the record I had to make as a pastor when the annual report was due. I was trying to mobilize the congregation to help me achieve my goal.

I can remember, with deep humiliation now, how I secretly longed to have a larger congregation than the Baptist Church (the largest Protestant church in town) and the envy I felt when I compared their beautiful and more spacious facilities with our meager Presbyterian plant. The sense of competition grew and deepened though I never would have admitted it at the time. I found myself becoming actually jealous because of the success especially of the Baptist pastor. How I found myself exulting when we established a larger youth group than the Baptist church. And I took great pride in the fact that we were reaching more of the leadership in the high school. (As a matter of fact, that was not because of me; the former pastor had done such a splendid job with junior high and they had now moved into senior high).

This hidden agenda must also have communicated with those I tried to reach in the community. From their point of view they must have felt I was trying primarily to get them into First Presbyterian Church. I worked harder than ever to get the congregation to see its responsibility for reaching into the community and for evangelizing all ages. I'm afraid I exhorted and scolded much more than I instructed in those days of putting undue pressure on the congregation.

This even affected my longing for revival. From my earliest days in the Lord I was exposed to men and women who longed to see revival in the church and I cannot remember when I did not long for revival. This desire for revival was not entirely pure and selfless. Revival would mean an awakened congregation, an awakened congregation would mean a greater outreach in the community, a greater outreach in the community would mean more converts and that would be a growing membership which would eventually require a larger plant and result in a larger benevolence budget. This ambivalence must have infected everything I did in those days.

Meanwhile something else was happening. I became increasingly aware of the time I had to spend on institutional matters: committee meetings, office administration, mimeographing of the church bulletin, programming (especially for youth activities), getting young people to camps and conferences, arranging for transportation. This was, of course, in addition to the pastoral duties which I began to believe ought to be shared by the congregation. As yet, I had not learned how to guide them into ministering. These institutional activities were preventing me from being with people.

During my third summer as pastor of the church in Coalinga, I had a life-changing experience while at a Sunday school conference at Forest Home, California. A fresh visitation of the Holy Spirit came upon a small group of us while we were at prayer. This changed my life radically. Subsequently discussions with those who shared this experience with me led to the decision that the conventional pastorate was not my calling and that I should devote myself completely to reaching people where they lived daily without the pressures of getting them to join a church. Accordingly a series of deep, thoughtful, prayerful conversations with the session of the church led to my decision. I had their genuine cooperation and approval to resign as a pastor. The resignation was consummated three months later in a very wonderful spirit of love and encouragement. As a matter of fact, the last week in that church I conducted an evangelistic meeting with great blessing.

At that time I had no plans for the future. It seemed agreeable with all concerned that I remain in the little community and develop a ministry to people where they lived and worked daily. I would devote my time entirely to being with people wherever there was opportunity and to serving them as the need seemed to indicate.

God had other plans. Dr. Louis H. Evans, Sr., of the First Presbyterian Church of Hollywood, invited me to be one of his assistants with the understanding that I would be free to develop this nonconventional ministry in any way that the Spirit of God seemed to lead in the Los Angeles area. The agreement was that I would be under no obligation to bring people into the Hollywood First Presbyterian Church. Instead, in the name of Christ and the church I would minister to people wherever there was opportunity and whatever direction they might go so far as church life was concerned as a result of this ministry. This was to be an experiment for one year after which we would evaluate and decide whether or not it was right for me to continue on the staff of the church in Hollywood. The experiment resulted in my remaining on the staff of that church for eight and a half years before moving to Washington, D.C. to be associated with International Christian Leadership (the Prayer Breakfast Group movement which had begun in Seattle, Washington in 1935).

In the early spring of my third year at the church in Coalinga the desire to disciple men led to a weekly breakfast group in the church. The reason that the breakfast hour was chosen was practical inasmuch as the men laid on my heart to disciple were all busy men. Generally their lunch times were taken with business and their evenings were quite often as filled as were mine. The most available time to get these men together was at breakfast. One of the men had to be at work at 8 o'clock in the morning so we decided to meet at the church for breakfast every Wednesday at 6:30. A woman in the congregation was kind enough to come to the church early Wednesday morning and prepare this breakfast for twelve of us. We had committed ourselves to meet together every Wednesday at 6:30 A.M.

for three months which was providential, for I am sure that if we had not, the breakfasts would not have lasted for more than a few weeks.

Those early meetings were exceedingly interesting for all of us. I did not come prepared to speak. The men expected me to speak inasmuch as I was a clergyman and this is what clergy did. My desire was to study the Bible inductively with the men, to depend upon the Spirit of God to lead us together to discover what He had caused to be recorded in the book of Romans. The first morning we read the first seventeen verses and then I asked the men to comment on what they had read. Absolute silence prevailed. It was apparent that they expected me to tell them what the passage taught, and I was anxious for them to share their impressions. The silence was embarrassing but we were committed to stay together. Our first day in Romans was not very fruitful but we had some laughs and we got to know each other a little better and some of the invisible walls that separated us were dissolved. Briefly at least we removed our masks and were our real selves with each other. The second week was better. They did not come expecting me to teach a Bible lesson and they understood that we were to read the passage and comment on what we saw in it. The comments were interesting and varied and as we continued to meet over the weeks it was absolutely amazing the things we discovered together in the book of Romans.

We learned many things in that first breakfast group. First of all, as we sat together week after week, we grew to know one another at increasingly deeper levels. We came to love one another and to really care and be concerned about our brother's spiritual welfare as well as his family and his work. In our prayer times we found ourselves more anxious to support one another with intercessory prayer not only at the breakfast but throughout the week. Thus this deep, wonderful friendship developed. I learned the meaning of being with men—just *with* them. It was at this time that the text in Mark 3:14 came to mean much to me. It is recorded that, "(Jesus) ordained twelve, that they should be with him and that he might send them forth." The preposition "with" came to have great meaning for me as I comprehended slowly a significant fact. Jesus Christ loved the masses; the whole world lay heavily upon His heart; He had come to redeem the whole world; His ministry was to be brief. Still He deliberately devoted much of His three years of public ministry to only twelve men. He was with them under all kinds of circumstances. It was supremely important to Him to be "with" them.

In fact, this was Jesus' theological seminary for the apostles. His strategy was simply to be with them. They grew to know one another, to be patient with one another, to care for one another, to love one another, to support one another, to dare to be critical and to help one another change. All the time they were growing in their knowledge of Jesus Christ. They were not just learning things about Him but they were learning to know Him, to feel Him, to absorb His attitudes and feelings, to learn by example as well as by parable and precept.

Up to that time I was never with a man unless I had some purpose, either to bring him to some kind of a decision for Christ, to get him to do something for the church or to get him to give money to some worthy activity. Now I began to realize that it was important to be with men just to be with them.

I will never forget an experience early in my time at the First Presbyterian Church of Hollywood. There was a man in the congregation whom I admired greatly at a distance. I wanted to know him. One Sunday morning I asked if we could get together. He invited me to his club downtown for lunch on Tuesday. We met at the appointed time, 12:30, and had a wonderful lunch together. At about twenty minutes to two he looked at his watch and said, "Now, Dick, I have a 2:00 o'clock appointment at the office and have to leave in about ten minutes. What did you want?" I said I didn't want anything; I just wanted to be with him. He got the strangest look in his eye and said to me, "Come on Dick, we're friends—you can level with me—do you want some money for the church? Do you want me to do something? What do you want?" I said, "Honestly, I just wanted to be with you." He was silent for a minute and then he said, "Dick, this is the first time in my life that a preacher wanted to be with me when he didn't want something from me."

Here is that insidious commercial spirit again which so easily communicates non-verbally to people. Even when we want to win them to Christ, they feel like objects to be reached rather than persons to be loved and cared for. They feel like a statistic. As one person put it, "You just want my soul to hang on your belt." Decisions for Christ become a kind of conquest. We find ourselves wanting to report our triumph to our friends, to let them know how many we have led to Christ. Or if our purpose is not evangelism, they begin to feel that the only time we are with them is when we want something from them. Either we need their financial support for some program we are doing or we want them to get involved with one of our plans. In one way or another it seems we are with them to use them for our purposes. We are mobilizing people for our programs and this is exploitation however worthy our objective. I learned in that first breakfast the deep satisfaction of being with men just for the pleasure of their company.

Something else became quite apparent. As we studied the Bible together and learned to know one another better and developed a mutual concern and sense of support, evangelism happened. Some of the men in that original breakfast had never opened their heart to Jesus Christ but as a result of that breakfast, they met the Savior. They began to grow and without any pressure to make any kind of decision, just in the fellowship of that weekly breakfast, every one of those men developed in his own way into an effective disciple for Jesus Christ.

Also, I learned that I needed those men as much as they needed me. The Spirit of God taught me a great deal through those laymen. I knew the Bible better than they. I had studied in a seminary and had a theological orientation. I was the professional, but time and again the Spirit of God revealed things to them in the Scriptures that were edifying to me personally. I needed their prayers, I needed their care and their love, and I began to realize that laymen could minister to me as effectively as I could minister to them, as a matter of fact, perhaps more effectively. But also as they ministered to me I became increasingly effective in my ministry. It was then in a very real sense a team ministry. Whatever God was doing through me was partly because of what those men were doing to me and with me in ministry and in fellowship.

I learned what true *koinonia* is and the importance of fellowship in the church. The first epistle of John, especially chapter 1, began to have great

significance for me in my ministry. I began to
see that the great burden of the epistles, as a
matter of fact, the burden of our Lord's teaching
to His apostles, was not their outreach to the
world but their responsibility to one another as
disciples. I saw evangelism as a natural outgrowth
of fellowship and then Acts began to open up
to me in a completely new way. The heart of
that rapid and extensive expansion of the Apostolic Church was a community which had been
born at Pentecost, a community of people who
although they were human, sinful and weak, loved
one another, cared for one another, needed one
another, ministered to one another, supported one
another. The community itself in that violent,
hostile, alienated world was a testimony to the
reconciliation in Christ which was being preached
by the apostles and witnessed to by individual
disciples. The quality of the life of this community was attractive and compelling like an
oasis in a barren desert. By their love for one
another they demonstrated to the world of un-
believers that they were disciples of Jesus Christ.
Their unity was a supernatural phenomenon in
that divided, decadent civilization. Their care for
one another, their service to one another testified
to the jaded culture of the Roman Empire that
something utterly new and fresh and radical had
happened. The unbelieving world was attracted
to this amazing little community. Without any
of the organization, the buildings, the prestige,

the wealth, the position that the contemporary church knows, they became known as those "who turned the world upside down." My way of thinking about the church began to change radically.

THE SCATTERED CHURCH

You are the salt of the earth; but if salt has lost its taste, how shall its saltness be restored? It is no longer good for anything except to be thrown out and trodden under foot by men.

(Matthew 5:13)

The following is extracted from a personal letter written by the chairman of one of the agencies of the federal government. He is writing about a man he had met for the first time. Recently awakened to new interest in Christ, he expresses perfectly a way of thinking about the church:

> He is the kind of fellow who makes me feel ashamed. He is so busy with God's work that if I didn't know better I would believe that this is his full-time job. Come to think of it, it is his full time job and therein lies the secret for all of us. In business, with our families and yes, even at golf, we can be busy with God's work. It should not be a Sunday thing or even a prayer group thing but rather a constant way of life. What a challenge!

Chapter 9

The Scattered Church

Where is your church? Generally we answer this question by giving the address of the building where worship and Sunday school are conducted. Conventionally the building is spoken of as the "church" and people think of the church in these terms. Or church is the peculiar activity which takes place inside a building with a peculiar type of architecture (much effort has gone into designing buildings that don't "look like" a church) at peculiar times in the week. This activity involves songs which are sung at no other time, prayers that are made at no other time, and words that are spoken at no other time.

In the minds of many there is absolutely no connection between what occurs in the church on Sunday and what goes on in the community the rest of the week. This is true unless the organi-

101

zation of the church or churches takes some kind of a "stand" regarding a particular issue and makes known this stand to the press. Another way the members of the church give visibility to their stand is by marching or demonstrating, or writing in the "readers write" department of newspapers and magazines. Or they may boycott some business operation.

Thinking this way about the church puts the ecclesiastical establishment at the center—whether it is a building (whatever the architecture) or an organization or a program. The church becomes just another community pressure group which is able to do as much or more or less for the improvement of the community as the service clubs, welfare organizations, etc. that have proliferated for such purposes.

Thinking this way about the church involves its members irresistibly in the building or the organization of the program. The implication is that the larger and stronger and more efficient the establishment becomes, the greater the pressure she will be able to exert in the proper places and the wider her influence in the community. Her influence is always and exclusively that of the ecclesiastical establishment. Those outside the church measure her influence, her relevance to the affairs of the community in terms of her corporate impact on those affairs.

On the basis of such thinking about the church her influence in the world is minimal, hardly worth mentioning. An exception, of course, would be the influence of the Roman Catholic Church with her great worldwide organization, her powerful hierarchy and the enormous prestige of the Pope and the Vatican. Also worthy of mention in this regard are the various international and national church councils which have had some impact on national and international affairs. Certainly these have given "visibility" to the church in the last twenty-five years.

But—is this the church? And is this the sum and substance of her influence in the world? Is her maximum influence organizational, corporate, unilateral?

There is another way of thinking about the church which is expressed in an uncommon answer to the question, "Where is your church?" Most of the week the church is not at the address where she worships; she is scattered all over the community, in hundreds of homes, schools, offices and markets, etc. Church does not stop with the benediction Sunday morning. It does not cease to be the church when not gathered, when scattered throughout the city. She does not cease to be the church when she is invisible as a corporate form.

Our Lord gave two analogies which help to show the authentic influence of the church in the world. He said, "Ye are the salt of the earth." Salt, left in a shaker, its grains gathered together and visible as salt, is useless. To serve its purpose,

103

it must be scattered and when it is scattered it disappears into the food. When salt is doing its work, it is invisible. And incidentally, when the meal is over, it is not the salt which is remembered, but the delicious food which the salt made palatable.

Both of the parables regarding seed attracted the attention of the disciples when our Lord taught them (Matthew 13) and He explained both to them. The second is akin to the analogy of the salt. "The Son of Man is the sower, the field is the world, and the good seed are the children of the kingdom" (Matthew 13:37-38).

In its gathered, visible form in the granary, seed is useless. To serve the purpose for which it exists, it must be scattered, it disappears into the soil and literally dies. When seed is doing the work for which it was intended, it is invisible.

Think of the church in this scattered, invisible form, penetrating the social, economic and political structures of the world between Sundays. Think of the potential of this dispersion, multiplied millions of disciples, scattered throughout the world, planted by the Son of Man in millions of acres of the field which is the world, disappearing like salt and seed into the substance, the soil of the life where they live and labor between Sundays.

What an incredible strategy our Lord envisioned in the analogies of the salt and the seed. Think of the impact upon every phase of worldly life by these children of the Kingdom when they accept where they are as the place where Christ has sowed them. Think of the implication of considering what they do where they are as Christ's sacred calling and vocation for them. Think of their penetrating, growing influence when they accept their situation as the will of God for them unless and until He relocates them and/or calls them to another task. Think of their influence as they do this in the love of God and in the power of the Holy Spirit with a deep sense of their accountability to Christ—and do it to the glory of God.

But you say, unfortunately millions of Christians do not think that way or live that way. Precisely! They have probably been taught to think that only as they do something in and for the church establishment are they doing the work of the church; only as they do something "religious" are they really serving Him. And most are so busy making a living they have only marginal time to do anything for Christ or the church.

So they go through life suffering low-grade frustration because they are unable to serve Christ "full time" as their pastor or the missionary or the evangelist does. The best they can do is give money to subsidize the "full time" workers to serve Christ while they are forced to devote themselves most of the time to a "secular" pursuit. What a tragic caricature of New Testament discipleship!

105

What is the program of your church? Here is another common question which invariably evokes the conventional answer about ecclesiastical or religious involvement. "We have a large and active Sunday school, several excellent choirs, a vigorous men's fellowship and women's association and a going youth program." The program of the church is thought of as what is done in and for the religious institution, what takes place at that address where the people gather a few hours a week.

As has already been suggested, it takes relatively few of the members of the church to run the program of the church. Perhaps ten percent of the people, more or less, are needed for Sunday school, choirs, ushering, official boards, and various organizations within the church establishment. If that is the work of the church, most members are without any opportunity for such activity. Here again many suffer low-grade frustration as year after year passes and they are never elected to office or invited to "do anything for the church."

Think of it this way. The program of our church is everything all the members are doing between Sundays. The church keeps house, goes to school, teaches, practices law, medicine and dentistry, runs business and industry, farms, works on construction jobs, researches in many fields, sits on school boards, city councils, county councils, state legislatures and congress. Between Sundays the church is involved in everything productive and constructive that is happening in the community. And it does so as a witness to Christ, to the glory of God, in His love and in the power of the Holy Spirit, sensitive to its accountability to Christ.

And what of the church work which is done in and for the church organization? Its purpose is to equip each member to do the work for the church Monday through Saturday. All the programs within the church are for the purpose of enabling the church to do the work of ministry between Sundays when she is invisible as a congregation.

This requires every member of the church. Every member ought to be engaged in full-time service for Jesus Christ!

WHERE DO YOU BEGIN?

So we are ambassadors for Christ, God making his appeal through us. We beseech you on behalf of Christ, be reconciled to God.

(2 Corinthians 5:20)

Chapter 10

Where Do You Begin?

"But I can't relate to *every*body," the pastor declared in some anger and frustration. He was really saying that therefore he could not develop a close relationship with *any*body.

We were in a discussion which concerned the importance of relationships as essential to equipping the church for ministry in the world. The not uncommon idea that a minister and his wife cannot cultivate any close friendships was being upheld. The assumption was of course, that if a pastor and/or his wife had any close friends, these people would be considered as "pets" or "favorites." Therefore, close personal relationships were impossible for the pastor.

What did our Lord think about this? Mark records (3:14) that, "Jesus chose twelve ... to be with him, that he might send them forth...."

With the whole world for which He was to lay down His life on His heart, and three short years of ministry, our Lord deliberately gave Himself much of the time to only twelve men. He never lacked a crowd, nor did He ignore them. He always had compassion on the crowds and He ministered to them again and again. Nevertheless, He reserved His deepest, plainest teaching for the twelve, and He devoted most of His time to them, often withdrawing from the crowds to do so.

Furthermore, within the twelve there were distinctive relationships. John was known as "the beloved." It was he who lay his head on Jesus' chest at the last supper, who, when the others wanted an answer, asked Jesus. Peter, James and John were invited to accompany Jesus to the mount where He was transfigured and also into the Garden of Gethsemane during the profoundest moment of His earthly life before His crucifixion. And Peter seemed to get some special attention at the seaside breakfast following the resurrection (John 21).

Apparently Jesus believed that the best way to reach the world was to train twelve men and the best way to train them was simply to have them with Him as much as possible. The preposition is important—they were *with* Him in most of the circumstances of life. They heard what He said, saw what He did, but more important they felt what He was in those months of close fellowship with Him. They were involved in the most intimate aspects of His life and were able to learn, not only by precept and example, but by the far greater nonverbal, nonvisual impressions which they absorbed unconsciously through these months.

And they were not only learning what Jesus was like, they were learning to know each other at his worst as well as his best. The twelve were growing together, learning how to love one another, honor one another, serve one another, encourage and instruct one another, criticize one another, confess their sins to one another, pray for one another. They were learning life in community. They were being prepared to become the core of the new community which was to be born at Pentecost.

The way Jesus used to reach the world was to devote Himself to twelve men. It is impossible to improve on this strategy.

Of course a pastor cannot develop close, intimate relationships with everyone, but he can with a few and he will be effective in equiping the many for ministry if he gives himself to a few for the sake of ministry. At all cost he must guard his relationship to Jesus Christ. Obvious as this is, one of the easiest things a pastor can do is to neglect a personal relationship with Christ. And it is so easily justifiable because he has so many things to do for Christ. But all else will suffer if he does not guard and strengthen his

113

relationship to Christ through regular devotional practices.

His wife and family come next. This is also an obvious truth. Yet how often a pastor's wife and family are neglected for the sake of the work. The casualties of such neglect are legion and unspeakably tragic. The nearest human relationship to that between Christ and His church is the unity of a man with his wife (Ephesians 5:21-33). Therefore a pastor is not benefitting the church he serves if he neglects wife and family in the process. Ultimately the work will suffer as well as the home.

Next comes his associates in those churches where there is a multiple ministry. Here again the obvious is often tragically neglected. Far too often the senior pastor maintains only a professional relationship with his associates. They spend little time with each other and when they are together, there is always the agenda which keeps their relationship professional and never allows it to be personal. Rare is the multiple staff where pastor and associates enjoy intimate and personal relationships, a fact which is incalculably costly to the church. Jesus had time for a few men; no pastor can justify neglect of those who work with him in ministry.

Then there are the officers of the church. They have a right to the time and interest of the pastor —more time and more deeply personal interest than is possible at official board meetings with that omnipresent agenda. They have a right to be with the pastor for no other purpose than being with him.

Jesus did not use textbooks or manuals to train the twelve. He spent time with them, allowed them into the most intimate experiences of His life. This is not to exclude textbooks or manuals as teaching tools, but it is to say that they are no substitute for spending time with people.

Give yourself to a few and the many will benefit. Devote yourself to a few, molding their lives to the extent you are able by presence as well as precept, and you will be most relevant to the greatest number in preaching, teaching and all other activities.

As you communicate, nonverbally as well as verbally, to the few with you, they will in turn be communicating with others around them and the fellowship will be extended throughout the congregation and out into the world.

As fellowship with Christ is nurtured, one's wife and family benefit. As fellowship with one's wife is nurtured, the children and outsiders benefit. Christ-like relationships with a few benefit many. And conversely, estrangement in the relationship with the few adversely affects the many.

As Jesus incarnated the Word so must we enflesh the reconciliation we proclaim. As it was costly to Jesus, so will it be to us who take reconciliation seriously. The price is in pride, personal

115

interest, self-centeredness. But the rewards in friendships and blessing to others are incalculable. The cost is to let go of things we hold dear that we may grasp that which is dearest. For the "pearl of great price" the wise man sells all.

> Do nothing from selfishness or conceit, but in humility count others better than yourselves. Let each of you look not only to his own interests, but also to the interests of others. Have this mind among yourselves which you have in Christ Jesus, who, though he was in the form of God, did not count equality with God a thing to be grasped, but emptied himself, taking the form of a servant, being born in the likeness of men. And being found in human form he humbled himself and became obedient unto death, even death on a cross.
>
> Philippians 2:3-8

We were traveling to a leadership seminar in Boston. A member of our team, a black brother, handed me a copy of *Ebony* Magazine, opened to an article on black-white coalition movements in history. The author traced the progress of various coalitions since before the Civil War, discussed their failures and the reasons for them. One of his conclusions excited the team inasmuch as it confirmed our collective experience over the past ten years. He wrote, "Coalitions cannot be negotiated, they must be forged...." He described forging as involving the hammer and the heat.

Human relationships are not automatic, they involve struggle. But it is the struggle that seasons and strengthens the relationship. Love to be strong requires exercise.

Our tendency is to presume upon our personal relationships, expect them to work out of their own accord. Often we learn too late that indifference and neglect of a relationship allows it to disintegrate. Far too easily we capitulate to difficulty in this area and lose the relationship, however important it may be.

We neglect worship, prayer, Bible study, and fellowship, then wonder why our love for God cools off and the Christian experience becomes remote and unreal. Not that the Heavenly Father ever forsakes us—His love is constant and unrelenting—but when we fail to abide in Him, our lives grow lukewarm and unfruitful. It was their devotion to doctrine, fellowship, breaking of bread and prayer which kept the faith of the Apostolic Church hot and contagious.

In marriage this fact is tragically apparent. Young couples, blindly in love, assume their relationship will persist without difficulty. Not realizing that disillusionment is part of the maturation process, they expect the honeymoon to last forever. As they wrestle with the adjustments common to all human relationships, they begin to question their love. At this point they must realize that the very struggles they encounter will continue but these struggles are the raw material

117

for a deepened, sweetened love. As muscle grows with exercise, so love matures with struggle.

The point is that many couples are unwilling to pay the price. Forgetting the unconditional contract for life they made in the presence of God and before loved ones and friends in the wedding ceremony, or in their naivete, they assume there is no hope for the marriage and decide separation and/or divorce are inescapable.

Here commitment is the key. They made a covenant when they began their life together. If that covenant is taken seriously, the problems they face together will nourish their love and tighten the bonds which made them one. In other words, separation or divorce are not options. Whatever happens, however difficult, the marriage must be sustained. Herein lies the harmony, poise and peace in the lives of those beautiful people who celebrate their golden wedding anniversaries.

All teamwork involves struggle. A large group turns out for football, competes for positions until the team is finally selected. Then they learn to cooperate to enjoy the fruits of victory against their opponents. The team learns how to handle inter-team jealousies, conflicts and rivalries, or they disintegrate.

Speaking at a conference in Colorado Springs some years ago, a vice president of I.B.M. was describing the learning process facing his company as it entered the computer field. He attributed their success to "team creativity." Heretofore they had isolated a man so he could think and be creative. As young engineers took over they struggled together in interdisciplinary teams to give I.B.M. its immense success in computer technology. Before the team creativity they defined leadership as anyone others would follow. They were forced to redefine leadership. They learned that a leader was one who could "generate, communicate and sustain commonality of purpose."

Determine to give priority to relationships with associates and officers in the church and you can expect struggle. But commitment to the priority of persons enables you to go through the struggles and discover deepened, strengthened relationships. Pride, jealousy, envy, self-pity, competition will manifest themselves, but do not capitulate. Expect this as part of the process whereby effective human relationships are forged. Pay the price and your reward is a fellowship which is inseparable and invincible.

Our Lord put up with all the foibles and eccentricities of the twelve. He did not let their struggle for position—not even the desire of the mother of James and John that they be given pre-eminence in the Kingdom—coerce Him to give up on the fellowship. He endured, taught, cared, led and loved. He even invited Judas to the memorable supper which instituted communion. He never excluded Peter even when he, despite his earnest resolution not to do so, denied

119

the Lord with oaths. Jesus chose them to be with Him and He stayed with them through all the painful exigencies of their collective pilgrimage.

When we disciple men like that the possibilities are absolutely immeasurable for ourselves, for our associates, for the Christian community and for the world. We will see the thrilling implementation of the Great Commission.